OUR
AMERICA

GROWING UP
IN
PIONEER
AMERICA

1800
TO
1890

JUDITH PINKERTON JOSEPHSON

Lerner Publications Company
Minneapolis

To Pat Hatfield, a tireless researcher, outstanding librarian, and true friend

Many thanks to Edith Fine, Melissa Irick, and the members of my critique group. My thanks also to the state historical societies in Oregon, Utah, Colorado, and Nebraska, and to the San Mateo County Historical Society, San Diego Historical Society, San Dieguito Heritage Museum, and Encinitas Historical Society. Thanks to my editor, Sara Saetre, for her vision for this series and her careful editing. I'm also grateful to the many children who recorded their experiences during the great westward migration, especially those who appear in this book.

Lerner Publications Company
A division of Lerner Publishing Group
241 First Avenue North
Minneapolis, MN 55401 U.S.A.
Website address: www.lernerbooks.com

Photographs and illustrations in this book are used with the permission of: Salmon D. Butcher Collection, Nebraska State Historical Society, pp. 5. 20, 28, 32; Hulton Archive/Getty Images, pp. 6, 17, 52; New York Public Library, p. 7; Scotts Bluff National Monument, p. 8; map illustration by Laura Westlund, p. 10; National Archives, pp. 10–11, 12, 16, 54 (Pacific Alaska Region); Denver Public Library, Western History Collection, pp. 13, 14, 40; James L. Amos, p. 18; Utah State Historical Society, p. 19; The Kansas State Historical Society, pp. 22, 36, 41, 55; Wyoming State Archives, p. 24; Fred Hulstrand History in Pictures Collection, NDSU, Fargo, ND, p. 26; Idaho State Historical Society, p. 29; Minnesota Historical Society, pp. 30, 48, 49, 56, 57; Laura Ingalls Wilder-Rose Wilder Lane Museum, Mansfield, Missouri, p. 31; San Diego Historical Society, p. 33; San Dieguito Heritage Museum, Traux Collection, p. 34; Library of Congress, p. 35; Montana Historical Society, Helena, p. 37; State Historical Society of North Dakota, p. 38; Oregon Historical Society, p. 39; Encinitas Historical Society, p. 43; Nebraska State Historical Society, p. 44; The Mark Twain Project, the Bancroft Library, p. 45; Courtesy of Judith and Kirsten Josephson, pp. 47, 59; Homesteader Museum, Powell, Wyoming, p. 51; Sutter's Fort State Historic Park, Courtesy of Niki Pahl, p. 53;
Front cover image: Salmon D. Butcher Collection, Nebraska State Historical Society.

Library of Congress Cataloging-in-Publication Data

Josephson, Judith Pinkerton.
    Growing up in pioneer America, 1800 to 1890 / by Judith Pinkerton Josephson.
      p.   cm. — (Our America)
    Includes bibliographical references and index.
    Summary: Drescibes what life was like for young people moving to and living on the western frontier.
    ISBN 0-8225-0659-9 (lib. bdg. : alk. paper)
    1.Frontier and pioneer life—West (U.S.)—Juvenile literature. 2. West (U.S.)—History—19th century—Juvenile literature. 3. West (U.S.)—Social life and customs—19th century—Juvenile literature. 4. Pioneer children—West (U.S.)—Social life and customs—19th century—Juvenile literature. 5. Pioneer children—West (U.S.)—Social conditions—19th century—Juvenile literature. 6. Overland journeys to the Pacific—Juvenile literature. 7. West (U.S.)—History—19th century—Sources—Juvenile literature. [1. Frontier and pioneer life—West (U.S.)—Sources. 2. Overland journeys to the Pacific—Sources.] I. Title. II. Series.
    F596.J63 2003
    978—dc21   2001006825

Manufactured in the United States of America
1 2 3 4 5 6 – JR – 08 07 06 05 04 03

CONTENTS

NOTE
TO
READERS

Studying history is a way of snooping into the past. To gather clues about the way people lived in a past time, historians read old diaries and letters. They look at old newspapers, magazines, and photographs. They study old tools, cooking utensils, and clothes. All these things from the past are primary sources.

While writing this book, the author used many primary sources. She studied life during the years when many Americans headed west as pioneers, starting in the early 1800s and continuing through the rest of the century.

Many books about this period are historical fiction. Historical fiction is a made-up story that is set in a real time. The people you will meet in this book are real. You'll discover

Photographs are primary sources that tell a lot about the past. This photograph shows a youngster helping to brand cattle in Milburn, Nebraska.

drawings and photographs of them. You'll find quotes from their diaries and letters. The quotes are printed just the way they were written, misspellings and all.

As you read, you'll notice many things that are different from modern times. For example, no paved roads existed across the western United States. Pioneers followed dusty paths across the prairie, traveling in wagons (with no brakes) pulled by oxen or mules.

By studying the primary sources in this book, you can do some snooping of your own. Your ideas about the past will add to our understanding of the brave youngsters and other people who led the way west.

CHAPTER ONE

WAGONS HO!

"Turn your face to the Great West and there build up your home."

—Horace Greeley, *newspaper publisher and western traveller, 1859*

In the late summer of 1848, Virginia Watson's father came home from town and made a surprising announcement. "I have sold the farm and we will go to Oregon," he said. Mr. Watson's plan was "a great sorrow to me," eight-year-old Virginia later wrote in her diary. "I dearly loved our home." Ahead of her, however, lay a giant adventure.

Virginia's family spent all that fall and winter getting ready. First her father paid to have four wagons built in nearby Springfield, Illinois. The wagons would carry Virginia, her parents, her brothers and sisters, and all their supplies. Next the Watsons prepared food for the journey. They made jams and jellies. They dried fruit and meat. Then they stored this preserved food in tins, glass jars, and pottery crocks. They collected clothes and bedding to take with them. Just before they left, they filled several huge barrels with drinking water. Fresh water would be hard to find on the trail.

IN THE WILDERNESS

The time came for the Watsons to leave. Young Virginia took one last look at her family's cozy house, its walk lined with flowers, and the hickory tree where she gathered nuts. She said good-bye to her friends,

Opposite: American pioneers push west across the plains, 1885. *Right:* Emigrants (pioneers) like Virginia Watson's family would have used this guide on the trail.

THE

EMIGRANTS' GUIDE,

TO

OREGON AND CALIFORNIA,

CONTAINING SCENES AND INCIDENTS OF A PARTY OF
OREGON EMIGRANTS;

A DESCRIPTION OF OREGON;

SCENES AND INCIDENTS OF A PARTY OF CALIFORNIA
EMIGRANTS;

AND

A DESCRIPTION OF CALIFORNIA;

WITH

A DESCRIPTION OF THE DIFFERENT ROUTES TO
THOSE COUNTRIES;

AND

ALL NECESSARY INFORMATION RELATIVE TO THE
EQUIPMENT, SUPPLIES, AND THE METHOD
OF TRAVELING.

BY LANSFORD W. HASTINGS,
Leader of the Oregon and California Emigrants of 1842.

CINCINNATI:
PUBLISHED BY GEORGE CONCLIN,
STEREOTYPED BY SHEPARD & CO.

her aunts, and her cousin Molly. Other relatives and friends rode alongside the Watsons for several miles, then turned back. "We had to bid them farewell," Virginia wrote. "It was like a funeral."

The Watsons traveled on, passing farms and towns as they followed unpaved country roads. Melting snow and spring rains had turned some roads to mud. The wheels of their wagons sometimes sank into deep, muddy ruts.

Near Hannibal, Missouri, the Watsons reached the vast Mississippi River. "I had never seen so large a stream before," Virginia wrote. The family and their wagons crossed the river on a ferryboat. Then they continued across the state of Missouri.

When they reached the Missouri River near the city of St. Joseph, hundreds of people and their wagons were waiting to cross. When it was the Watsons' turn to drive across, Virginia worried that they might be swept into deeper water. "I thought we surely would all be drowned," she wrote.

River crossings could be treacherous. A wagon train crosses the south Platte River in Nebraska.

Safely on the other side, the Watsons joined a group bound for Oregon. No country roads stretched ahead of them. Instead, the group inched forward along winding, bumpy paths. As Virginia put it, "We were in the wilderness, and we were now really on our journey."

> "We were in the wilderness, and we were now really on our journey."
> —*Virginia Watson, 1849*

MADE TO LIVE IN

Pioneers like the Watsons had begun moving west of the Mississippi River in the early 1800s. Some sailed from the East Coast to the West Coast around the tip of South America. The trip meant spending months on rolling seas, cramped in a ship's cabin. Other pioneers traveled overland by train. But few railroad tracks had been laid. River routes across the continent were few, too.

Most pioneers traveled west in covered wagons. Most travelers took one of two main routes west, the Oregon Trail or the Santa Fe Trail. The Oregon Trail began at St. Joseph, Missouri, followed the Platte River, and crossed over the Rocky Mountains. The trail ended in what later became the state of Oregon. Some travelers went on to what would become Utah and California. The Santa Fe Trail began in Independence, Missouri, and headed west along the Arkansas River. One fork in the trail led to the area that became New Mexico, Arizona, and southern California.

By mid-century, wagon trains streamed across North America. Virginia Watson wrote, "From the Missouri River to where the road turned to California, we were never out of sight of long trains of covered wagons." Virginia's wagon train had fifty-two wagons in it.

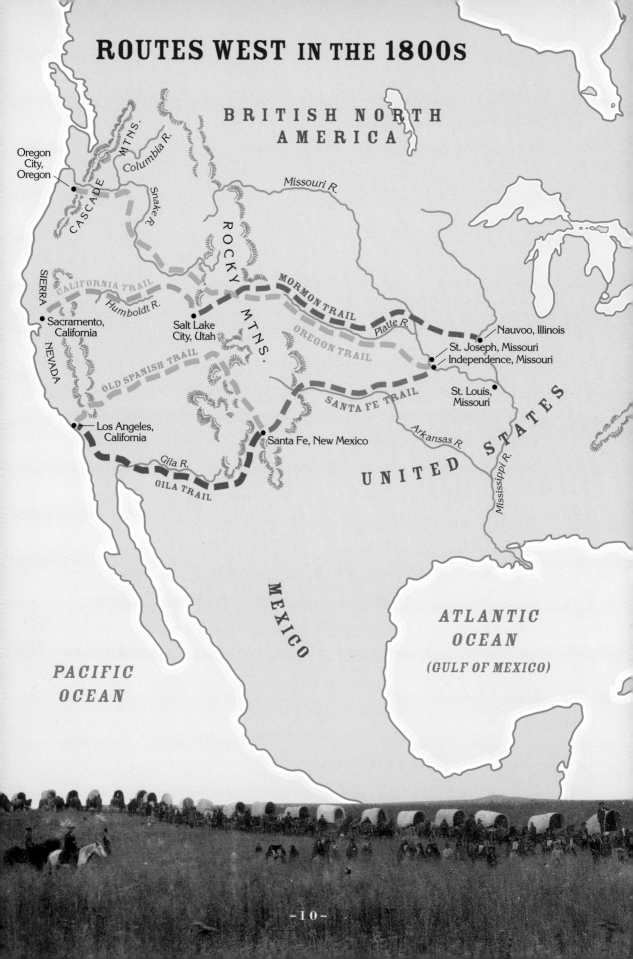

ROUTES WEST IN THE 1800S

BRITISH NORTH AMERICA

Oregon City, Oregon

Columbia R.

CASCADE MTNS.

Snake R.

Missouri R.

ROCKY MTNS.

CALIFORNIA TRAIL

SIERRA

Humboldt R.

Sacramento, California

NEVADA

MORMON TRAIL

Platte R.

OREGON TRAIL

Salt Lake City, Utah

OLD SPANISH TRAIL

Nauvoo, Illinois

St. Joseph, Missouri

Independence, Missouri

SANTA FE TRAIL

St. Louis, Missouri

Los Angeles, California

Gila R.

GILA TRAIL

Santa Fe, New Mexico

Arkansas R.

UNITED STATES

Mississippi R.

MEXICO

ATLANTIC OCEAN (GULF OF MEXICO)

PACIFIC OCEAN

A wagon train trip to the West Coast lasted four to seven months. Trips usually began in early spring. That way pioneers had enough time to finish the trip before snow began to fall in the Sierra Nevada and the Rocky Mountains. Covered wagons were huge—twelve to fourteen feet long. Wagons were "made to live in," as Virginia Watson put it. The wagon's roof was made by stretching a big sheet of canvas over curved hoops. People climbed inside through openings in the front and back.

A wagon could carry as much as five tons. Pots and pans and other supplies were hooked to the outside. Inside, the bottom was covered with boxes and chests filled with clothing, dishes, and tools. Stashed near the back were an iron stove, washtub, and crocks of food. Layered on top of these items were blankets, pillows, and cloth mattresses filled with horse hair or goose feathers. Teams of four to eight mules, oxen, or draft horses pulled the wagons. Girls and boys as young as eleven drove the teams. Some had practiced driving for months. When the weather was dry, swirling dust covered everything. Drivers could barely see the horns of their oxen.

In the 1800s, wagon trains streamed across North America west of the Mississippi River like columns of ants.

APPALACHIAN MTNS.

Pioneers brought house and home with them on the trail. This covered wagon is loaded with furniture, a butter churn, spinning wheel, and other daily necessities.

A wagon team had to work hard to pull its heavy load. To spare their team, many pioneers walked instead of riding. Only very young, old, or sick people rode. Passengers sometimes shared the wagon with baby pigs or chickens in coops. Saddle horses and cows trotted beside the wagon.

Wagons traveled up to twenty-five miles a day. A day spent traveling ten miles was a "ten-miles day." On July 9, 1878, Pamela Francis Loomis, age thirteen, described one hard day's journey. "We upset the buggy and brook [broke] the wheels off the left side," she wrote. "We traveled 21 miles today."

The day's travel usually ended by late afternoon. The travelers stopped, unyoked their teams, and drew their wagons into a circle. Often they pitched tents in the middle of the circle. Guards (some of them boys of eleven or twelve) kept watch through the night.

Each morning the travelers took down their tents, fixed breakfast, and loaded their wagons. The signal to leave came by seven o'clock. "Wagons ho!" shouted the driver of the lead wagon. Whips cracked. Oxen leaned into their yokes. Walkers stepped into place alongside the wagons. Slowly the long line of wagons rolled forward, and another day on the trail began.

ONE LONG, MOVING ADVENTURE

With each mile, pioneer children were leaving familiar people and places farther behind. They didn't know what lay ahead. Sometimes they shivered in their wagons or tents at night, listening to strange sounds in the dark. Panthers and mountain lions screamed. Nighthawks screeched. Wolves and coyotes howled.

A pioneer family stops to rest during their long journey westward.

Children often made new friends in their wagon train. But sooner or later, wagon train friends had to part, when their families chose different paths along the way. Once parted, they usually never saw each other again.

Little children didn't always understand where they were going or why. One campsite often looked just like the next. One little girl thought her family's wagon train was going in circles. Sobbing, she said they would never get to Oregon if they kept returning to the same camp each night.

Probably many pioneer children were more excited than afraid. Grassy plains, rugged mountains, and dense forests filled the landscape ahead. On the broad, flat prairie, herds of buffalo thundered past. Prairie dogs sat on their haunches and peered at passing wagons. Snakes and lizards slithered under rocks. Walking

To conserve the energy of the wagon teams, many children and adults walked instead of riding, which made for a long day.

"Dear Diary"

No matter how or when children reached the West, they had stories to tell in their diaries. Their diary entries tell a lot about their hopes, hardships, and daily lives. Samuel Terry McKean was seven when his family left Illinois for Oregon in 1847. In Oregon, he wrote, "anyone could get all the land he wanted for the taking." When Maude Baumann and her family arrived in Minnesota, she complained to her diary, "I can't hardly write on account of the mosquitoes. They're bigger than elephants." Oregon had mosquitoes, too. To escape them, Samuel McKean and his family spent nights floating on big a flatboat in the middle of a stream.

along to the music of thudding hooves, squeaking wheels, and jangling pots, the trip often seemed like one long, moving adventure.

PROMISES AND AN INDIAN PRINCESS

Many different Native American tribes lived in the West in the early 1800s. When pioneers and Native Americans met, children on both sides stared at each other with curiosity. The Indians watched pioneer children form letters in the sand, do embroidery, or sing songs. Often Native American people helped pioneers, sharing food or showing the best places to cross rivers.

Young Eliza McAuley and her family camped at Bear River in Utah for a week in July 1852. They made friends with a Native American named Poro and his young son. Poro's wife made deerskin moccasins for Eliza's whole family. Eliza wanted to give Poro's son her plaid shawl in exchange. But the boy asked for bread and sugar instead. As he explained, his hungry family could not eat the shawl.

An Apache girl. Native Americans and pioneer children knew little about each other's cultures.

Kate McDaniel, ten, traveled west in 1853. Along the way, she met the teenage daughter of a Dakota (Sioux) chief. The teenage girl wore a loose, white buckskin dress, fringed at the bottom, over long leggings. "She was about fifteen years old and . . . very beautiful," Kate wrote. "The little princess, as we liked to call her, let us pet her pony and then she showed us how she could

TRAIL OF TEARS

Beginning in the early 1800s, the U.S. government forced many Native American tribes to leave their homes in the East. The Seminole, Chickasaw, Choctaw, Creek, and Cherokee people all had to move to reservations (land set aside for them) in Indian Territory west of the Mississippi River.

In 1838 about fifteen thousand Cherokees began a move that was later called the Trail of Tears. One U.S. soldier described the beginning of the trip. "I saw them loaded like cattle or sheep into six hundred and forty-five wagons," he wrote. "When the wagons started rolling, many of the children . . . waved their little hands good-bye to their mountain homes." During the 1,200-mile journey to Indian Territory (present-day Oklahoma), some four thousand Cherokees died of disease and starvation. This number included many children.

A Pawnee family stands outside their lodge in Nebraska, 1871. Native Americans were forced out of their homes and onto reservations as pioneers settled Indian Territory.

ride and what her pony could do. . . . Then [she] jumped into her saddle, waved her hand to us, and with a little giggling laugh, was gone like a beautiful bird."

Beginning in the 1820s and 1830s, the U.S. government made promises to let Native Americans live freely on western lands. As more and more pioneers pushed into Indian Territory, however, the government broke many of those promises. It sent U.S. soldiers to protect pioneers who wanted to settle on Indian lands. Sometimes battles broke out between the soldiers and Indian people. Many Native Americans, U.S. soldiers, and pioneers were killed.

The fighting didn't stop settlers from streaming into the West. When enough white people had settled in an area, they worked to form a new state in the United States. Between 1850 and 1896, the nation gained fourteen new states. For most Native Americans, life was never the same again.

CHAPTER TWO

DANGERS
OF THE
TRAIL

"We arrived in Salt Lake City at nine o'clock at night. . . . My mother was dead in the wagon."

—Mary Goble, age thirteen, 1856

Why did so many families leave home and face the hardships of the journey west? The reasons were as different as the people were.

Gold drew many. In 1848 gold was discovered at Sutter's Mill in Sacramento, California. The Gold Rush began as people rushed to California, hoping to get rich.

Other people were looking for religious freedom. Members of the Church of Jesus Christ of Latter-day Saints, called Mormons, were

Opposite: A stone marks the grave of Lucinda E. Wright, who died on the Oregon Trail. *Above:* Mormons moved west, seeking religious freedom.

sometimes attacked for their beliefs. One Mormon leader, Joseph Smith, was even killed. Between 1847 and 1869, about seventy thousand Mormons left their homes in the East. They journeyed westward one thousand miles or more. Most settled in what later became the state of Utah.

Many Mormon pioneers had no covered wagons. They walked, pushing handcarts heaped high with their belongings. Nine-year-old John Stettler Stucki helped push his family's handcart west in 1856. John was often "so tired I would wish I could sit down for just a few minutes. . . . But instead of that, my dear, nearly worn-out father would ask me if I could not push a little more on the cart."

African Americans fled west from southern states, which allowed slavery. In some parts of the West, escaping slaves could be free. California and Oregon joined the United States as free states in 1846 and 1850. Kansas followed in 1861. After the Civil War, which ended in 1865, all slaves in the United States were free.

The Shore family moved to Custer County, Nebraska. The West offered freedom to many African Americans.

ONE RAINY NIGHT

One night in 1843, a sudden thunderstorm woke Jesse Applegate. The eight-year-old had been sleeping in a flimsy tent. "The rain was pouring down into my face," he later wrote. "My eyes were blinded with the glare of lightning, the wind was roaring like a furnace, and the crash of thunder was terrible." Jesse's uncle scooped him up "and put me into the hind end of a covered wagon," Jesse wrote. "In the morning the little river had overflowed its banks and the encampment was flooded."

FINDING FOOD AND WATER

Moving west meant freedom to some. But it did not mean an easy life. Many pioneer children had never lived outdoors. On the trail, their families had to cook on their small iron stoves or over open fires. No one could get warm on chilly days.

At first, travelers ate food they had brought along. Bacon or salt pork with dried apples made a good lunch. When travelers stopped to rest, they cooked hot meals on their stoves. People were careful with supplies such as shortening and flour, which couldn't be replaced. Children helped by gathering wild onions and herbs along creeks and in woods and ravines. They picked chokecherries, winter grapes, and "creek plums."

Most boys and girls had to know how to shoot a gun. Sometimes they hunted rabbits, quail, wild turkeys, and deer for food. But youngsters also needed guns for protection. Knowing how to shoot meant being safe from wild animals.

Finding water was another big job. The maps that wagon trains followed didn't give clear directions about where to find water.

A young boy carries a rifle. Children were expected to help hunt game for their families on the trail.

While parents did other jobs, children often traveled several miles on horseback or on foot in search of springs or creeks.

At times, pioneer children went hungry. Sometimes supplies fell out of wagons as wagons crossed streams. When pioneers passed through Indian lands, tribes often demanded food as payment. After many weeks on the trail, some weary travelers had nothing to eat but flour and water, rawhide (a kind of raw leather), or even tree bark.

"Nearly all the children would cry themselves to sleep every night."
—*Heber Robert McBride, 1856*

Heber Robert McBride was eight when his family moved west in 1856. He remembered, "Nearly all the children would cry themselves to sleep every night my 2 little Brothers would get the sack that had flour in and turn it wrong side out and suck and lick the flour dust."

A RIGHT WAY TO HUNT

In Native American tribes, men and boys did the hunting. Fathers taught sons how to study animals, identify their footprints, and hunt and butcher them. "There was a right way to cut up an animal and a right way to pack it on the pony," wrote Luther Standing Bear, a Dakota boy. Luther killed his first buffalo at age eight.

"NO ONE COME TO HELP ME"

The hard journey west made people weary. Many fell ill with diseases such as cholera. Cholera caused diarrhea and a high fever. People didn't know they could catch cholera by drinking polluted water. Flies buzzing around the soiled bedding of a cholera victim spread the disease to more people.

Many people died. Some children lost both parents and found themselves alone. Children died, too. By 1859 the major routes west were marked by ten graves per mile.

One mother wrote in her diary about her sixteen-year-old daughter. The girl was sick and knew she was going to die. She begged her mother to dig a grave at least six feet deep. "She did nat [not] want the wolves to dig her up and eat her," her mother wrote.

Families also worried that Indians without warm clothes might dig up bodies of loved ones to steal the dead persons' clothes. To hide new graves, people built campfires over them. Then they drove wagons through the ashes. That way, the ground did not look like a freshly dug place. In areas of hard soil and rock, people couldn't dig graves. They buried bodies under piles of rocks instead.

When tragedy struck, children often helped to hold their families together. Elizabeth Pulsipher was ten when her baby sister died on the journey west. Elizabeth's mother was sick. "I had to bathe her [the baby] and put a little dress on her, and sew a cloth around her body to be buried in as there was no coffin," Elizabeth wrote in her diary. "As small as I was, no one come to help me and mother was not able to do anything."

"As small as I was, no one come to help me and mother was not able to do anything."
—Elizabeth Pulsipher, mid-1800s

In 1856 thirteen-year-old Mary Goble and her family set out from Iowa for Utah, one thousand miles away. As they traveled, the weather grew freezing cold, and the Goble's food ran low.

These graves were covered with stones to keep the bodies from being dug up.

"I Thought We Would All Die There"

William Hockett was nine when he and his family left their home in Salem, Iowa, in 1847 to begin the long trek to Oregon. Near Fort Laramie, Wyoming, William and his father watched a group of about three hundred Pawnee warriors celebrate a victory over a group of Dakota Indians. As the Pawnee warriors jumped, twisted, and danced by firelight, William suddenly realized that the warriors were carrying sticks that had Dakota scalps dangling from the ends. "If ever a boy wished to be somewhere else," he wrote, "I was certainly that boy."

William had an older sister and brother, ages sixteen and fourteen, and a younger brother who was just a toddler. On the journey, both of their parents died of typhus. The children buried their parents in unmarked graves along the trail. William's older sister took charge of her three brothers. "How my sister escaped a nervous collapse is more than I have ever been able to understand, out in the wilds with three little brothers and one a baby...," William wrote. "Small as I was I thought we would all die there, and I almost hoped we would all die together." But none of the Hockett children died. Once they got to Oregon, William's older sister found homes for each of them with different families.

They used the little flour they had left to make a thin soup called skilly. They spent several days without fresh water. When Mary went to search for water, she got lost. By the time she was found, her feet and legs were frostbitten. "They carried me to camp. . . ," Mary wrote. "The pain was terrible." Doctors later amputated Mary's toes.

A Mormon family, the Gobles looked forward to their journey's end in Utah. But Mary Goble's baby sister and brother died on the trail. "We arrived in Salt Lake City at nine o'clock at night the 11th of December 1856 . . . ," wrote Mary. "My mother was dead in the wagon."

Children took over all the work when their parents fell ill or died. When young Heber Robert McBride's parents got sick, the exhausted oxen could not pull them. "The team was give out intirely [entirely]," Heber explained. Heber, his older sister Jenetta, and his younger brother Peter emptied the gear out of their parents' carts and added it to their own. "We had to take more load on our carts," he wrote, "and had to haul Father and Mother."

A pioneer family mourns at a child's funeral.

Mrs. McBride was sick most of the way. So Jenetta took over. "Jenetta had the worry of us children," Peter wrote. "She carried water from the river to do the cooking. Her shoes gave out, and she walked through the snow barefoot, actually leaving bloody tracks in the snow."

One day Heber went looking for his father. "At last I found him under a wagon with snow all over him and he was stiff and dead," wrote Heber. "I felt as though my heart would burst I sat down beside him on the snow and took hold of one of his hands and cried oh Father Father there we was away out on the Plains with hardly anything to eat and Father dead."

"There we was away out on the Plains with hardly anything to eat and Father dead."

—*Heber Robert McBride, 1856*

With their old homes far behind them and their families pushing endlessly ahead, pioneer children had few choices. They had to be as brave, daring, and strong as they could be. They could not quit. They had to go on.

CHAPTER THREE

LITTLE HOUSE
ON THE
PRAIRIE

"Oh, give me a home
where the buffalo roam."

—from "Home on the Range," a pioneer song

At the same time that some pioneers were traveling west, others were already starting to settle there. Probably for most travelers, the day they stopped traveling was a happy day.

Many pioneers settled on land without another house in sight. Families lived in their covered wagons while they built a hasty shack to protect themselves from wind and rain and wild animals. Then they gradually built a larger, more permanent house. Children helped with the work.

In wooded areas, pioneers built log cabins. But the vast, flat prairie had few trees. So settlers built houses made of thick blocks of soil called sod. The tangled roots of prairie grass held the soil together. The roots were so thick and tough that sod had to be cut with an iron plow.

The prairies could be blistering hot in the summer. But the dark inside of a sod house stayed cool. In winter a woodstove heated the house. The thick sod walls held in the warmth.

Opposite: A tidy sod house in Custer County, Nebraska.
Above: In areas where trees grew, pioneers built log cabins.

In 1899 nine-year-old Victoria Wilkinson's father built a house in Sheridan County, Nebraska. It was made of sod and wood. Its walls were four feet thick. As a finishing touch, Mr. Wilkinson smeared mud on the walls inside. The dried mud coating kept out wind.

Victoria and her sister often sat curled up in their home's deep windowsills. All five of the Wilkinson children slept in an upstairs loft. They had no real beds, just slabs of wood on the floor. Victoria's parents and the baby slept in a bed downstairs.

During long, hot summers, swarms of grasshoppers swooped down on the fields around the house. The pesky bugs chewed entire crops down to the bare stalks. Some grasshoppers usually managed to get inside the house. Spitting a brown juice, they clung

"Only the chickens liked the grasshoppers."
—*Victoria Wilkinson, 1899*

Swarms of grasshoppers plague a Minnesota farm.

to the lace curtains. Children called the grasshopper spit "tobacco juice," because it looked like the juice from chewing tobacco. "Only the chickens liked the grasshoppers," Victoria wrote later, because the chickens could eat them.

Prairie winters were harsh. Howling blizzards piled snowdrifts up to the roof. Laura Ingalls Wilder (the author of the Little House books) grew up in pioneer times. She remembered the

Laura Ingalls, *right,* with her sisters, Carrie, *left,* and Mary, *center*

rugged winter of 1881 in DeSmet, South Dakota. From December until May, deep snow kept trains from reaching town. Flour couldn't be shipped in. So people ground wheat in their coffee grinders to make flour. For fuel, they burned prairie grass braided into ropes.

FARMWORK

Once their houses were built, families planted crops. They cut down trees and brush to clear a field. They hacked at hard-packed soil with knives, picks, or axes. After planting rows were dug, children walked along the rows, dropping seeds into the holes by hand.

As soon as plants sprouted, the battle with birds began. To scare birds away from eating new plants, children ran up and down the rows, flapping their arms.

Edna Matthews Clifton hated picking cotton on her family's cotton farm in Texas. As she worked under the hot August sun, the shimmering fields stretched endlessly before her. "Sometimes I would lie down on my sack and want to die," Edna wrote. "They would pour water over my head to relieve me."

Before and after school, children milked cows and gathered eggs. At night they watched for coyotes that might attack the chickens. When winter covered everything with ice and snow, children carried baby animals inside so they wouldn't freeze to death.

Seventeen-year-old Nellie Nichols and her brother Clarence grew up on a ranch near Denver, Colorado, in the 1880s. Sometimes the family's livestock wandered off. "Clarence hunted for the horses again, did not find them. I am affraid they are gone for good," Nellie told her diary.

Like other pioneer girls, Nellie helped her mother cook, sew, and tend the garden. Doing the wash took days. Bedding had to be soaked in kerosene to kill bugs before being washed. Clothes had to be boiled, soaked, and scrubbed on a washboard, then beaten with a "battling stick" to smash out the dirt. Nellie had "an awfull big washing" one day in 1885. She told her diary, "I am too tired to write."

A young girl named Alice Butcher milked the cows on her family's farm in West Union, Nebraska.

Downtown Encinitas. To get around, people walked, rode a horse, or drove a horse and buggy.

SETTLING TOWNS

"Come to Encinitas" read an 1880s ad for this small oceanfront town near San Diego, California. The town needed more people. To encourage people to move there, the ad promised mild, sunny days and plenty of land.

The Noonan family saw the ad in a Colorado newspaper and took the train to Encinitas. In 1888 they built a blufftop home overlooking the ocean. Little Ida Noonan was three.

By the 1880s, pioneers had settled on farms and in small towns all over the West. Encinitas was a typical town. It had a hotel, a bank, and several stores.

Irish and Spanish people and many others added variety to life in Encinitas. The town's name came from the Spanish words *las encinitas*, which means "little live oaks." Spanish settlers also gave a Spanish name to the San Dieguito Indians, the area's original inhabitants.

Ida's father worked as a mine inspector. The West had copper, silver, and coal mines in addition to gold mines. Mr. Noonan made sure mines were safe for miners. Sometimes he traveled for months at a time. When Mr. Noonan was home, he and Ida took walks and watched the sun set over the ocean. He taught her to spell. He had lots of interesting ideas. Some day, he said, people would ride in machines that could fly like birds. Other machines would play music at home.

The weather in Encinitas was often dry. A strong wind could turn one spark into a raging fire. One December night, Mr. Noonan woke to the smell of smoke. He opened the door to the kitchen and faced a wall of flames. Quickly, he turned, wrapped Ida and her mother in blankets, and pushed them out the bedroom window.

"I awoke standing on the ground with my doll in my arms," wrote Ida, who was eight by this time. Ida's older brothers and sister weren't home. They returned to find their family's home burned to the ground.

The Noonans had lost a lot. Their furniture had been just as nice as any back East. There had been a marble-topped table and chairs made of black walnut and cherry wood. There had even been a black ebony piano. The Noonans had to find another place to live. But like many other hardy pioneers, they were just glad to have survived.

Ida Noonan and her family lost most
of their belongings in a fire.

"GOODBYE, GOD"

In 1879 one eleven-year-old girl learned that her family was moving to Bodie, California. The people in Bodie had a reputation for being wild and wicked. The young girl dreaded her new life in this rough-edged mining town. "Goodbye, God," she wrote in her diary. "I'm going to Bodie."

Colorado and other western places were bursting with mines and the towns that grew up near them. Coal mines employed

A trapper boy. Trapper boys worked long hours underground, tending mules in dangerous coal mines.

many young boys. "Breaker boys" worked long hours sorting valuable coal from worthless rubble. "Trapper boys" worked underground tending the mules that hauled carts of coal. Few children worked underground in gold mines. Instead they dipped fine-meshed sieves into rivers, sifting for gold dust and nuggets.

Youngsters in towns hawked newspapers and delivered groceries. Boys as young as fifteen ran ferries on local rivers, hunted and sold game, and delivered milk. Girls cleaned hotel rooms and cooked for boarders.

In many families, youngsters scrubbed floors with white creek sand, using a mop made from corn shucks. They scoured brass utensils with salt, vinegar, and ashes.

ORPHAN TRAINS

Some children in pioneer days lived in orphanages on the East Coast. Some were orphans. Others had parents, but their parents couldn't care for them. Beginning in 1859, a charity group called the Children's Aid Society sent thousands of these children west on trains to find new homes. Adults from the society traveled along.

Ads posted in pioneer towns announced that a group of orphan children was coming. A notice in Tecumseh, Nebraska, read: "10 BABES: Boys and girls from one month to three months. One boy baby, has fine head and face, black eyes and hair, fat and pretty; three months old."

When orphan trains pulled into towns, people interested in adopting these children gathered to meet them and choose one. Some orphans found warm, loving families. Others were taken by families who treated them like servants. By 1929 more than 200,000 children had found new homes in this way.

Geneva Fornell gathers water for washing, cooking, and drinking. Most pioneer children had to help their families survive by getting jobs or doing chores at home.

Other chores included canning fruits and vegetables. Youngsters also helped with smoking meat and churning butter.

Some pioneer children didn't have to work for money. In established towns, wealthy families hired servants to do most household work. But even a wealthy child had home chores. By chopping wood, wiping dishes, or doing other chores, children learned the value of work.

Most pioneer children had no choice but to work. Youngsters who helped support their family could feel proud. Sometimes their work meant the difference between life and death.

CHAPTER FOUR

READIN', 'RITIN', AND 'RITHMETIC

"23 pupils in a house 10 x 12, dirt floor & no door!"

—Angeline Brown, *a pioneer schoolteacher*

Children traveling in wagon trains didn't get any formal education. Some read books whenever they could. Pioneers packed along as many books as they could. When a wagon's load needed to be lightened to cross a river or a mountain, many families left behind clothes or household goods. They rarely discarded precious books.

EARLY SCHOOLS

Setting up a school took time and money. Taxes to pay for public schools were not common. So the children in many frontier towns did not have a school.

No laws made parents send their children to school. Even in places with a school, not all children attended. Some youngsters went to school for only half the year. They spent the remaining months helping their parents.

In the 1850s, Comfort Elizabeth

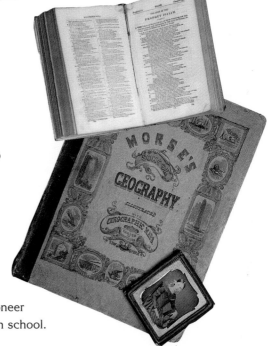

Opposite: A pioneer classroom. *Right:* Pioneer children used books like these while in school.

Godfrey learned her ABCs at home from a printed card. She also practiced writing the words imprinted on the family's metal stove.

Students in Denver practice a reading lesson.

Her younger brothers and sisters went to school. But as the oldest child, she had to help her mother.

Sometimes several families pooled their money to hire a teacher. Teachers in the West were often promised twice what they could have earned back East. They didn't always get the money, though. After four months of teaching, one Oklahoma teacher had been paid only two dollars. The rest of his salary was paid with six chickens, a pig, and the meat from one-fourth of a cow.

COUNT YOUR CHANGE

To learn math, pioneer children often worked problems based on real life. *The New Practical Arithmetic,* a math book published in 1887, asked students to find the cost of the following items, using multiplication.

  5 pair of opera glasses @ $9
  7 velocipedes [bicycles] @ $8
  6 tons of coal @ $7
  12 lbs. of cheese @ $.09
  9 lbs. of figs @ $.12
  7 oranges @ $.07

In rough cowboy towns, almost anybody could be a teacher—including barmaids, peddlers, and strangers passing through. Teachers like these didn't teach much. They promised only that they would not get drunk during school hours. In other places, some lucky children had well-educated teachers who taught Latin or classical literature along with reading, writing, and arithmetic.

Like other schools in the United States, most frontier schools were one-room schoolhouses. A school could be a dimly lit cabin or an abandoned sod house. An old rug covered the dirt floor. Gunnysacks covered the walls. Children sat on hard benches, boxes, or the floor. When children had to go to the bathroom, they ducked behind a rock or a tree. Some schools were fancier. They had outhouses (outdoor bathrooms), blackboards, factory-made desks, and extras such as maps, globes, and book collections. Coats hung on hooks in a coatroom.

Students of a one-room schoolhouse gather outside their
sod school building in Kansas.

Between five and twenty-five students attended a one-room school. Students as young as five and as old as sixteen all studied in the same room. Usually the room was noisy. Teaching was a challenge, especially for young teachers.

In Ida Noonan's school, students sat in one big room. On foggy winter days, everyone huddled around the potbelly stove in the middle of the room. Students brought lunches from home in a tin pail. Outside, a cistern (a covered cement tub) collected rainwater that ran off the roof. When students were thirsty, one of the larger boys dipped a bucket into the cistern. Then everybody took turns lowering a dipper into the bucket.

CAN'T CHAW TOBACCO

Paper was expensive and hard to get. Often students wrote on a slate (a small chalkboard). They quickly learned how to make a piece of chalk squeak on their slates. Children wiped slates clean with a wet cloth or sponge, or just spit.

Schools often didn't provide books. So students sometimes brought their own. Sometimes several children shared one book. A textbook that included many different subjects was called a reader.

Youngsters at the Encinitas schoolhouse studied grammar, literature, spelling, and science. They also did "mental arithmetic"— adding numbers in their heads. The problems weren't easy. (Try multiplying 17 times 22,458 in your head.) Some afternoons, children climbed down the bluff to do their lessons by the ocean. On Fridays they recited a memorized poem or essay.

As an adult, Laura Ingalls Wilder lived with her husband and child on a Missouri farm. On school days, Laura's daughter, Rose, rode her donkey, Spookendyke, to a school in a nearby town. Rose was

Students and teachers from Encinitas sometimes had class on the beach.

too short to fit in the big desks at school. "My feet ached from dangling," Rose later wrote.

A poor girl from the country, Rose Wilder's lunch pail held only an apple and slices of brown bread spread with bacon grease. "We were too poor to have butter," she remembered. She longed to make friends with the town girls, but "all of them turned their noses up at me." Rose envied the town girls' "wonderful dresses . . . trimmed with satin and velvet, and big hats with ostrich feathers on them, and gold-plated bracelets." Town girls also "chewed gum and curled their hair and were always simply throwing nickels away on candy and new tablets [notepads]."

"We were too poor to have butter."
—Rose Wilder

Like some modern schools, Rose's school had spelling contests. Rose was a good speller. "It was my one chance to feel superior to the town girls," Rose said. "They might laugh at my clothes but they couldn't laugh at my spelling. However, they [the town girls] didn't care about spelling."

INDIAN BOARDING SCHOOLS

By the late 1800s, most Native Americans had been forced to move to reservations. The U.S. government sent many Native American children to boarding schools *(below)* run by the government. The children had to live away from home. They were forced to cut their long hair, trade in their own clothes for white people's clothes, and stop speaking their native language. Sometimes the classrooms seemed more like jails than schools.

California pioneers forced out not only Native Americans but also Mexican people who had lived there for generations. (Until 1848 California was part of Mexico.) Newly arrived California residents refused to grant Mexican people rights as citizens. Sometimes Mexican children were not even allowed to attend school.

Fifteen-year-old Samuel Clemens. Samuel learned how to be a printer before becoming famous as an author. He used the pen name Mark Twain.

Samuel Clemens, who became famous as author Mark Twain, attended a one-room school in Illinois in the 1840s. His classmates valued practical skills—such as being able to chew tobacco—more than school subjects, such as spelling or math. When Samuel started school, "A strapping girl of fifteen, in the customary sunbonnet and calico dress, asked me if I 'used tobacco.'" Samuel answered no. Shocked at his lack of skills, the girl teased, "Here is a boy seven years old who can't chaw [chew] tobacco."

HANGING ON A PEG

Punishment followed quickly if children misbehaved in school. They weren't allowed to whisper, fight, squeak chalk across their slates, or forget their lessons. Some offenders had to wear tall, pointed dunce caps and stand in front of the class. Others were sent to the coatroom. Some teachers spanked students or rapped their knuckles with a birch switch (a branch). One Utah teacher punished students who misbehaved by hanging them on coat pegs by the backs of their clothes.

SCHOOL PUNISHMENTS

At Mason Street School in San Diego, California, children earned lashes for bad behaviors such as these.

Boys and Girls Playing Together	*4 lashes*
Fighting at School	*5 lashes*
Giving Each Other Ill Names	*3 lashes*
Wearing Long Fingernails	*2 lashes*
Scuffling at School	*4 lashes*
Calling Each Other Liars	*4 lashes*
Swearing at School	*8 lashes*

In the late 1850s, Martha James Cragun attended school near Salt Lake City, Utah. When one of her classmates misbehaved, he had to hang by his feet from one of the ceiling beams until his face got red and his eyes bulged. Watching him, Martha and the rest of the children cried. Later, Martha's older brother Elisha twisted a girl's hair. The teacher threatened to stick Elisha's head in the stove and burn his hair off. Martha clung to the teacher's knees, begging for mercy for her brother.

LEARNING AT HOME

When pioneer children couldn't go to school, they read whatever was at hand. Sometimes this meant reading the same things their parents read. Youngsters liked *The Life of Daniel Boone*, since it was an adventure book about the Wild West. Other favorites were the Bible, *Robinson Crusoe*, *Pilgrim's Progress*, and works by Sir Walter Scott, William Shakespeare, and Charles Dickens. In some frontier communities, young people had newspapers to read. Magazines published long stories chapter by chapter.

Pioneers used kerosene lanterns like this one to light their way outside at night.

Families frequently read together. Ida Noonan's father often read to his family as Mrs. Noonan ironed. Young Ida heard the novels *Twenty Thousand Leagues under the Sea*, *Around the World in Eighty Days*, *The Count of Monte Cristo*, and Shakespeare's works.

Rose Wilder's family made a nightly ritual out of reading. Her father made a big pan of popcorn after supper. Then her mother read out loud by the light of the kerosene lantern. Rose curled up with her dog, Fido. "It was the cozy, comfortable hour for all of us," Rose later wrote. "We had had supper, the room was warm, we were alone together, the horses fed and sleeping in the barn, nothing to worry or hurt us till tomorrow and Mama . . . was reading. That was best of all."

CHAPTER FIVE

SLEIGH RIDES
AND
FIREWORKS

"We would fly over the snow, as he cracked his whip and shouted at his horses."

—Horace Hall Cummings, Provo, Utah, writing about the driver of a winter sleigh ride, 1860s

Pioneer children had no electronic games or other modern toys. They used their imaginations and their outdoor world for play. At day's end on the trail, children scrambled around each new campsite, eager to explore. Each place held surprises such as hairy tarantulas, skittering centipedes, and sidewinding snakes. They chased butterflies, beetles, and scrawking prairie chickens.

Sarah Sophia Moulding, age three, looked forward to stopping for the night. "We girls would get out and play with a little girl in the next wagon, who had a set of [doll] dishes made of lead," she said later.

Jesse Applegate remembered "ox bouncing," a game he and other boys invented on the way to Oregon. Earlier travelers had killed an ox and left its empty stomach to rot in the sun. Swollen with gas, the stomach had puffed up as big as a barrel. Jesse and his friends took turns running and butting their heads against the bloated ox stomach. Each time, the boy bounced off. Then one boy took a flying leap at the target. It burst open, and the boy plunged headfirst into a squishy, smelly mess. The skin of the stomach closed tightly around his neck like a noose. The other boys had to grab his legs and pull him out.

CELEBRATIONS

On Valentine's Day, some children bought ready-made valentines with formal messages such as "Wilt thou be mine?"

Opposite: Fred Bailey with toboggan, 1876.
Above: Two girls host an elegant tea party, 1880s.

and "I adore thee." Other children made their own cards, using scraps of paper and ribbons.

On the first day of May, children danced around a maypole, a tall pole decorated with long ribbons. Each person held one ribbon. As children circled the pole, the ribbons wove around it. Ida Noonan and her friends filled May baskets with wildflowers. They hung the baskets on people's doorknobs, knocked, then ran away giggling.

The Fourth of July celebrated the signing of the Declaration of Independence and an expanding America. On July 4, 1859, teenager Maria Elliott wrote, "I was awakened this morning bright and early by the firing of guns from some distant companies.... They had not forgotten Independence Day [even] if they were far away on the plains."

On Halloween in Denver, Colorado, Bessie Thompson, seventeen, roasted chestnuts and played games with her friends. That day's diary entry said: "All Hallow's Eve.... We had such fun tonight."

Americans had celebrated Thanksgiving since colonial times. But Thanksgiving didn't become a national day of thanks until 1863. Even on Thanksgiving, food served in pioneer homes wasn't always

FIREWORKS!

Maude Baumann was in the parade in her town, Bagley, Minnesota, one Fourth of July. "I marched with the girls...right behind the band," Maude wrote. "Miss Bruster was the Goddess of Liberty....We saw those great fireworks....The men in the boat got their fireworks afire somehow. The boat looked almost exactly as tho [though] it was blowing up."

a feast. Laura Ingalls Wilder's family rarely had fresh meat during South Dakota's fall and winter. On Thanksgiving 1879, a flock of wild geese flew over young Laura's house. Her father hurried outside, shotgun in hand. Dreaming of roast goose, Laura and her sister argued about whether or not to put sage in the stuffing. Then their father

A frontier Thanksgiving in Powell, Wyoming

returned empty handed. Both girls realized that they would have welcomed a feast of goose, with or without sage stuffing.

In 1822 Clement Clarke Moore wrote the poem *The Night before Christmas*. After that, Santa Claus became part of Christmas traditions. Santa was pictured as a youthful bearer of gifts. By the end of the nineteenth century, he looked more like a kindly grandfather.

On Christmas Eve in 1883, Bertha Shaw and her brothers and sisters went to the nearby town of Pescadero, California, to see the big Christmas tree. Later, they hung up their stockings for Santa Claus to fill. On Christmas Day, Bertha wrote, "Mama got a pair of vaces [vases] papa got a shaving mug. The babies got a doll a piece I got a dress, stockings, can of nuts and a little box. Annie got a dress, a shawl, candy and nuts. John got some paints and a hanchief

Rocking horses were extravagant presents in pioneer America.

[handkerchief]. Edgar got a shirt."

On birthdays, children usually received simple, practical gifts such as a knife, a glove buttoner, or a lead pencil. On some lucky birthday, a child might get a rocking horse or a doll. John Cullen turned nine on June 18, 1847, en route to Oregon. He didn't get many presents, but he had fun anyway. "I celebrated by going fishing and had an exciting time catching a very large catfish," he wrote.

TOYS AND GAMES

Many pioneer girls stitched their own dolls. Alma Mineer was six years old when she traveled west. She remembered, "My older sisters used to make rag dolls as they walked along for us little children to play with. The faces had button eyes and painted or sewn mouths and noses and yarn for hair." Girls also created dolls out of socks, bottles, flowers, corn husks, even cucumbers and squash. Grass, corn silk, and scraps of fabric served as makeshift doll clothes.

Most pioneer children had played blindman's buff, pom-pom pullaway, ante over, ring-around-the-rosy, and drop-the-handkerchief. Some children played a version of hide-and-seek called all-the-tigers-are-gone. It was played in the dark. The child who was the tiger "stalked" about looking for the other children.

They darted from one hiding place to another. When the tiger found someone hiding, he ran to tag them. If they got caught, they became tigers, too, and helped the first tiger search.

Pioneers often had fun while they worked. Sometimes several families gathered to do big jobs such as husking corn or baling hay. A boy lucky enough to shuck a red ear of corn could claim a kiss from a girl. At quilting bees, visitors crowded into a log cabin or a sod house. The women and girls chatted as they quilted and sewed. Often someone told ghost stories by the fire. Outside, children whooped and hollered as they played hide-and-seek.

Families sometimes ended a long day with singing. Strains of this favorite tune often wafted out into the darkness:

Buffalo gals,
Won't you come out tonight,
Come out tonight,
Come out tonight?
Buffalo gals,
Won't you come out tonight,
And dance by the light of the moon?

"My older sisters used to make rag dolls as they walked along...."
—*Alma Mineer, 1861*

This tiny wooden doll, Dolly, belonged to a pioneer child named Patty Reed. She carried the doll all the way from Missouri to California.

CHAPTER SIX

GROWN
AND
GONE

"How far I've come! I'm the same girl and yet not the same."

—Caddie Woodlawn, a character in a novel by Carol Ryrie Brink

Fictional character Caddie Woodlawn grew up fishing, climbing trees, and doing things boys usually did. As Caddie grew older, her father encouraged her to give up her tomboy ways and be a "lady." "It is the sisters and wives and mothers . . . who keep the world sweet and beautiful," he explained. "What a rough world it would be if there were only men and boys in it, doing things in their rough way."

Mr. Woodlawn is a made-up character. But many pioneer parents felt the same way. Girls practiced "women's work." They embroidered quilts and played with dolls. They learned to sew, knit, and cook. Boys rode hobbyhorses, chased rabbits, and twirled lassos. They learned how to rope cattle and build houses. On the frontier, many girls did those things, too, especially when the men and boys weren't around.

Not all "women's work" was pleasant indoor work. Here, Ada McCall gathers buffalo chips (dung) for fuel.

COMING TO CALL

Young people married early, sometimes as teenagers. The purpose of courting was to find a husband or a wife. On the trail, a boy "came to call" at a girl's wagon, just as he might have visited her home back East. Margaret Gay Clawson was seventeen when she went west in 1849. She felt "as much at home sitting on an ox yoke as if I were sitting in a parlor in an easy chair. Such is life on the plains," she wrote.

The westward journey gave many young people more freedom to socialize. Boys and girls strolled, arm in arm, or rode double on horseback. A fiddled tune or the strumming of a banjo or guitar brightened singing and dancing around a campfire.

"[I felt] as much at home sitting on an ox yoke as if I were sitting in . . . an easy chair."

—*Margaret Gay Clawson, 1849*

Nettie Spencer grew up in Oregon in the 1870s. Courting often took place at the all-day church meetings she attended, as people visited, picnicked, and listened to sermons. "When a boy would get old enough for a wife," Nettie wrote, "the father would let him use the horse and buggy for a trip to the camp meeting to get him a wife."

Young people also met at dances, plays, or concerts. At box socials, girls brought decorated lunch boxes filled with special foods. Boys drew numbers or bid money to share a girl's lunch. Francis Washington Kirkham, seventeen, attended one box social in Utah. "It was a draw party...," he wrote. "I had the very good luck to draw Miss Laura Hickman."

A young boy gets his hair trimmed before the Saturday night dance.

WEDDING BELLS AND SHIVAREES

Many men settled on their land before they married. In the 1860s, the government had passed the Homestead Act. If a man claimed some land (up to 160 acres), built a house and barn, and lived there for five years, the government gave him the deed to (ownership of) the land. Some "homesteaders" advertised for brides in East Coast newspapers.

This formal wedding portrait was taken in St. Paul, Minnesota, in 1883.

Victoria Jacobs was in love when she celebrated her seventeenth birthday on June 28, 1856, in San Diego, California. She wrote in her diary, "Received the congratulations of my brothers and sisters. But the congratulations of my betrothed [the man she was to marry] was sweeter than any." Like many young women of the time, Victoria married an older man. She died at age twenty-three after giving birth to her third child.

Mary Patton Taylor's parents fell in love on the trail and married when they reached Oregon. Mary's father split rails to earn the $2.25 he paid the preacher. Mary's mother started keeping house with one plate.

Friends sometimes gave newlyweds a "shivaree" (a noisy nighttime serenade). Rebecca Nutting remembered one shivaree in a wagon train. "Most of the men and women in the company took hold of

APACHE WEDDING BLESSING

Now you will feel no rain
For each of you will be a shelter to the other.
Now you will feel no cold,
For each of you will be warmth to the other.
Now there is no loneliness for you.
Now there is no more loneliness.
Now you are two bodies,
But there is only one life before you.
Go now to your dwelling place,
To enter your days together.
And may your days be good
And long on the Earth.

the wagon, the men at the tongue [front poles] pulling, the women at the back pushing, and ran the wagon a half mile out on the prairie. Then the fun began. Such a banging of cans, shooting of guns, and every noise conceivable. . . . The disturbance was kept up until midnight."

MOVING ON

When pioneer boys grew up, some worked as farmers, surveyors, lawyers, businessmen, and lumberjacks. Jesse Applegate, the boy who had played "ox bouncing" on the trail, reached Oregon with his family in 1843. In 1863 he married Virginia Watson, the little girl who had been so sad to leave her Illinois home. The couple had seven children.

Pioneer women rarely had a profession, except teaching. Some schoolteachers were almost as young as their students were. Maude

Baumann had just turned fifteen when she decided to teach the next year in northern Minnesota. Even though she was shorter than most of her future students, she thought she could control them. "I'd haf [have] to get me a 'Club' and wallop [spank] thier [their] skins, and tan thier hides if they wouldn't mind. . . ," she wrote. "Won't I be somebody. Everybody will take thier hats off to me."

The author's grandmother, Ida Lewis, traveled west in a covered wagon in 1880.

Ida Noonan became one of the few girls who went on to college. Her mother went along as chaperone. Later, Ida taught in the same Encinitas schoolhouse she had attended as a child. She married and had five children. Eventually she became a much-loved librarian in Encinitas.

Laura Ingalls Wilder, the mother of Rose Wilder, wrote books for children. Stories drawn from her childhood made pioneer life come alive for her readers. One of Wilder's books, *Little House on the Prairie*, became the basis for a popular television series.

Most children had no say in their parents' decision to move west. Yet children showed they could do anything—drive a team of oxen, find food and water in strange new places, and even bury their own parents. While some children did not survive, others grew up to lead long, useful lives. Without these brave boys and girls, the West would be a different place today.

ACTIVITIES

STUDY HISTORICAL PHOTOGRAPHS

Soon after photography was invented in 1839, photographers joined surveying teams as they mapped western lands. The photographs from these trips inspired Americans to travel and settle in the West.

The first camera equipment was big and clumsy. People had to stay still for as long as thirty minutes while their picture was being taken. Otherwise the picture would be blurred. Old-fashioned cameras and film needed plenty of light, so photographs were usually taken outside. All photographs of pioneers are black and white. Color film had not been invented.

As western towns sprang up, photographers set up business. "Get your picture taken before you die or look worse," read one ad. Pioneers wanted to send photographs of themselves back home to their relatives and old friends. They wanted to look their best in these portraits.

Look at the photograph on page 26. The coffin of a young child who has died is on a table, putting it at the center of this family portrait. Notice that everyone is wearing his or her best outfit. The girls and the youngest woman are wearing dresses with leg-of-mutton sleeves (puffy at the shoulder and tight below the elbow). This style was high fashion in the late 1800s. The family's house has glass windows, which were expensive and hard to get. Pioneer families were proud of their homes and often included them in family portraits.

When you study historical photographs, continue to ask questions such as Who took the picture? Who are the people in it? What are they thinking and feeling? Follow these steps to study other photographs and illustrations in this book. Then write what you think one of them means.

WRITE A LETTER

Pretend you are traveling west in a wagon train. Together with a friend, write letters to each other for two weeks. Explain why you are going west, who is traveling with you, and what you do for fun on the trail. Describe the dangers you've encountered and the sights you've seen. Then talk about how it felt to communicate with letters instead of using the telephone or e-mail.

INVENT A TOY

Pioneer children often made their own toys from materials around their homes. Pioneer girls sewed dolls or made corn husk dolls. In some Native American groups, youngsters created twirler toys out of sticks. You can make a toy with odds and ends of materials at your house. Try empty milk cartons, empty spools of thread, string, and so on. Learn how to make a corn husk doll at <http://www.teachersfirst.com/summer/cornhusk.htm>.

ASK LAURA INGALLS WILDER A QUESTION

Many children who read the Little House books by Laura Ingalls Wilder wrote letters to her, and she always answered. Some of the children's letters are kept at the Herbert Hoover Presidential Library and Museum in West Branch, Iowa. After Mrs. Wilder died, young readers still wanted to be able to ask questions about her and her books. So the library maintains a web page where people can e-mail questions. A librarian then e-mails an answer based on what is known about Mrs. Wilder. If you would like to ask a question, visit <http://www.hoover.nara.gov/kids/dearlaura.html> .

PLAY ANTE OVER

Most pioneer children knew the game ante over (also called Anti-I-Over or Annie-over-the-Shanty). Players needed to play near a barrier, such as a wagon or a big rock. You could choose a barrier such as a garage, a fence, or a tall hedge.

To play, have two teams (three or more on each team works best) line up on either side of the barrier. Then one team calls "Ante Over!" and throws a ball over the barrier. If the other team doesn't catch the ball, they throw it back with the same call. But if the other team does catch the ball, they run around the barrier and throw the ball at members of the first team. (Be careful not to throw the ball too hard.) Anybody who is hit joins the opposite team. The game ends when one team runs out of players. If the game has to end before then, the team with the most players wins.

Source Notes

6   Horace Greeley, *New York Tribune*, 1841.

7–11   Virginia Watson Applegate, 1849, "Recollections of Childhood, 1840–1852," manuscript #233, Portland, OR, Oregon Historical Society.

12   Pamela Francis Loomis, July 9, 1878, "Overland Diary," manuscript #35, Portland, OR, Oregon Historical Society.

15   Samuel Terry McKean, Jr., n.d., "Reminiscences of Overland Journey in 1847," manuscript #483, Portland, OR, Oregon Historical Society.

15   Maude Baumann, May 30, 1900, "Maude Baumann Diary," St. Paul, MN, Minnesota Historical Society.

16   Kate McDaniel, quoted in Emmy E. Werner, *Pioneer Children on the Journey West* (Boulder, CO: Westview Press, 1995), 167.

16   Unnamed army private, quoted in Geoffrey C. Ward, *The West: An Illustrated History* (Boston, MA: Little, Brown, 1996), 84.

19   Mary Goble, quoted in Susan Arrington Madsen, *I Walked to Zion* (Salt Lake City, UT: Deseret Book Company, 1994), 94.

20   John Stettler Stucki, quoted in Madsen, 54–55.

21   Jesse Applegate, *Westward Journeys: Memoirs of Jesse A. Applegate and Lavinia Honeyman Porter Who Traveled the Overland Trail* (Chicago, IL: Lakeside Press, 1989), 28.

22   Jill Jacobsen Andros, "The Story of Children on the Mormon Trail," *Beehive History* 22 (1996), 7–8.

23   Luther Standing Bear, *My Indian Boyhood* (Lincoln, NE: U. of Nebraska Press, 1931), 45.

23   Unnamed pioneer woman, quoted in Lillian Schlissel, *Women's Diaries of the Westward Journey* (New York: Schocken Books, 1982), 47.

24   Elizabeth Pulsipher, quoted in Andros, 8.

25   William A. Hockett, April 10, 1914, "Experiences of W. A. Hockett on the Oregon Trail 1847," manuscript #1036, Portland, OR, Oregon Historical Society.

26   Mary Goble, quoted in Madsen, 92–95.

26   Heber Robert McBride, quoted in Andros, 8.

27   Peter Howard McBride, quoted in Madsen, 45.

27   Heber Robert McBride, quoted in Andros, 7.

30   Queen Victoria Wilkinson Wager, n.d., "Diary 1898–1899," manuscript #1403, Lincoln, NE, Nebraska State Historical Society.

32   Edna Matthews Clifton, quoted in Elliot West, *Growing Up with the Country: Childhood on the Far Western Frontier* (Albuquerque, NM: University of New Mexico Press, 1989), 73.

32   Nellie Nichols, March 16 and April 17, 1885, [Diary], Denver, Colorado, Colorado Historical Society.

34   Ida Noonan Truax, n.d., "Memoirs 1888–1987," Encinitas, CA, Encinitas Historical Society.

35   Ward, 61.

36   Andrea Warren, *Orphan Train Rider: One Boy's True Story* (Boston, MA: Houghton Mifflin, 1996), 37.

40   Waite A. Shoemaker and Isabel Lawrence, *The New Practical Arithmetic* (St. Paul, MN: D. D. Merrill, 1887), 69.

43   Noel Rae, editor, *Witnessing America* (New York: Stonesong Press, 1996), 87–89.

45   Samuel Clemens, quoted in Rae, 81.

47   Rose Wilder, quoted in Rae, 90.

48, 49   Horace Hall Cummings, quoted in Susan Arrington Madsen, *Growing Up in Zion* (Salt Lake City, UT: Deseret Book Company, 1996), 53, 109.

50   Maria Elliott, quoted in Werner, 118.

50   Bessie M. Thompson, October 31, 1887, [Diary], Denver, CO, Colorado Historical Society.

50   Maude Baumann, July 4, 1900.

51–52   Bertha Shaw, December 24, 1883, [Diary], San Mateo, CA, San Mateo County Historical Society Museum.

52 John Cullen, n.d., "Reminiscences of an Oregon Pioneer April 21, 1847, to February 24, 1848," Portland, OR, Oregon Historical Society.
53 Alma Miner Felt, quoted in Madsen, *Growing Up in Zion*, 39.
54 Carol Ryrie Brink, *Caddie Woodlawn* (New York: Macmillan, 1936), 27.
55–56 Margaret Gay Clawson, quoted in Andros, 4.
56 Nettie Spencer, quoted in Rae, 316–317.
56 Madsen, *Growing Up in Zion*, 155.
57 Victoria Jacobs, *Diary of a San Diego Girl—1856* (Santa Monica, CA: Norton B. Stern, 1974), 25.
57–58 Rebecca Nutting, quoted in Werner, 117–118.
59 Maude Baumann, July 4, 1900.

SELECTED BIBLIOGRAPHY

Anderson, William T., editor. *Little House Sampler/Laura Ingalls Wilder, Rose Wilder Lane*. Lincoln, NE: University of Nebraska Press, 1988.

Applegate, Jesse. *Westward Journeys: Memoirs of Jesse A. Applegate and Lavinia Honeyman Porter Who Traveled the Overland Trail*. Chicago, IL: Lakeside Press, 1989.

Hampsten, Elizabeth. *Settlers' Children: Growing Up on the Great Plains*. Norman, OK: University of Oklahoma Press, 1991.

Hartley, Mac. *Encinitas History and Heritage*. Encinitas, CA: Encinitas Historical Society and the San Dieguito Heritage Museum, 2000.

Jacobs, Victoria. *Diary of a San Diego Girl—1856*. Santa Monica, CA: Norton B. Stern, 1974.

Madsen, Susan Arrington. *Growing Up in Zion*. Salt Lake City, UT: Deseret Book Company, 1996.

McClary, Andrew. *Toys with Nine Lives: A Social History of American Toys*. New Haven, CT: Linnet Books, 1997.

Rae, Noel. *Witnessing America*. Washington, D.C.: Library of Congress/Stonesong Press, 1996.

Schlissel, Lillian. *Women's Diaries of the Westward Journey*. New York: Schocken Books, 1982.

Standing Bear, Luther. *My Indian Boyhood*. Lincoln, NE: University of Nebraska Press, 1931.

Ward, Geoffrey. *The West: An Illustrated History*. New York: Little Brown, 1996.

Werner, Emmy E. *Pioneer Children on the Journey West*. Boulder, CO: Westview Press, 1995.

West, Elliott. *Growing Up with the Country: Childhood on the Far Western Frontier*. Albuquerque, NM: University of New Mexico Press, 1989.

FURTHER READING

Chu, Daniel, and Bill Shaw. *Going Home to Nicodemus: The Story of an African American Frontier Town and the Pioneers Who Settled It*. Morristown, NJ: Silver Burdett Press, 1994.

Cunningham, Chet. *Chief Crazy Horse*. Minneapolis, MN: Lerner Publications Co., 2000.

Duncan, Dayton. *The West: An Illustrated History for Children*. New York: Little, Brown, 1996.

Krohn, Katherine. *Women of the Wild West*. Minneapolis, MN: Lerner Publications Co., 2000.

Krull, Kathleen. *Gonna Sing My Head Off! American Folk Songs for Children*. New York: Alfred A. Knopf, 1992.

Meli, Franco. *A Cheyenne*. Minneapolis, MN: Runestone Press, 1999.

Miller, Brandon Marie. *Buffalo Gals: Women of the Old West*. Minneapolis, MN: Lerner Publications Co., 1995.

Naranjo, Tito S. *A Pueblo*. Minneapolis, MN: Runestone Press, 2000.

Public Broadcasting Service. *New Perspectives on the West*. <http://www.pbs.org/weta/thewest>.

Sandler, Martin W. *Pioneers: A Library of Congress Book*. New York: HarperCollins, 1994.

Temko, Florence. *Traditional Crafts from Native North America*. Minneapolis, MN: Lerner Publications Co., 1997.

ThinkQuest Inc. *Pioneer Life in America*. <http://library.thinkquest.org/J001587/>.

Trinklein, Mike, and Steve Boettcher. *The Oregon Trail*. <http://www.isu.edu/~trinmich/Oregontrail.html>.

Wadsworth, Ginger. *Laura Ingalls Wilder: Storyteller of the Prairie*. Minneapolis, MN: Lerner Publications Co., 1997.

INDEX